The Appendectomy Grin

The Appendectomy Grin

Prose Poems

Charles Rafferty

AMERICAN POETS CONTINUUM SERIES NO. 218

BOA EDITIONS, LTD. ❋ ROCHESTER, NY ❋ 2025

First Edition
23 24 25 26 7 6 5 4 3 2 1

Publications by BOA Editions, Ltd.—a nonprofit corporation under section 501 (c) (3) of the United States Internal Revenue Code—are made possible with funds from a variety of sources, including public funds from the Literature Program of the National Endowment for the Arts; the New York State Council on the Arts, a state agency; and the County of Monroe, NY. Private funding sources include the Max and Marian Farash Charitable Foundation; the Mary S. Mulligan Charitable Trust; the Rochester Area Community Foundation; the Ames Amzalak Memorial Trust in memory of Henry Ames, Semon Amzalak, and Dan Amzalak; and contributions from many individuals nationwide. See Colophon on page 103 for special individual acknowledgments.

Cover Art: "Untitled 15, 1990" by Carl Chiarenza
Cover Design: Sandy Knight
Interior Design and Composition: Isabella Madeira
BOA Logo: Mirko

BOA Editions books are available electronically through BookShare, an online distributor offering Large-Print, Braille, Multimedia Audio Book, and Dyslexic formats, as well as through e-readers that feature text to speech capabilities.

Cataloging-in-Publication Data is available from the Library of Congress.

BOA Editions, Ltd.
250 North Goodman Street, Suite 306
Rochester, NY 14607
www.boaeditions.org
A. Poulin, Jr., Founder (1938-1996)

For Wendy, Callan, and Chatham

Contents

The Problem With Mutability

I've been thinking about Nefertiti's missing eye, and there are nights my wife recalls that suggest I was somebody else. The juniper stump at the end of our driveway has finally dissolved after twenty years. I got rid of the tree because it was hard to see the oncoming traffic, but I was too cheap to pay for a grinding. When our parakeet escaped, I put his cage on the back porch and believed he wouldn't forget us after making the sky's acquaintance. That's how dumb I was, is what I'm trying to say. That's how full of hope.

Conversation Piece

After the honeybees die out, somebody will start selling bee boxes as coffee tables — conversation pieces, something to hold a chessboard in the modern American living room. The signs are not good. The caviar industry wants to know why there aren't more sturgeon, and we're at the point where selling permits to hunt elephants is supposed to be good for elephants. I have come to learn it is difficult to do what is right for my children. Meanwhile, the snowy egret lives on in my grandmother's hat — the one that, in a sense, has never gone out of style.

A Love Poem of Sorts

This morning I threw a stone at a butterfly as it floated toward the purple hydrangea. Had I taken care while aiming, I'm certain I would have missed. Now its beauty is open to my inspection, and I can rub away the powder of its yellow wings. After all these years, this is how I think of you if I think of you at all — my darling, my dead butterfly.

I Am Not Without Hope

Most mushrooms look terrible by the time I find them, and I can go whole months without spotting a planet in the sky above our house. Of course, certain colors occur only on the abdomens of insects. Even flowers are incapable of the damselfly's iridescence. But look over here — a doily of lichen spreads across a boulder as if it were my grandmother's end table. I am not without hope. By late November, the cows are eating the corn maze we had paid five dollars to wander through.

The Problem With Luxury

There was a time when whitewall tires were a luxury, and people used to dine on ortolan buntings — pickled in brandy and eaten whole. The fact that it was repulsive meant nothing. It was a way of gorging oneself on what others could ill afford. Lately, the rich have been buying glacial ice found floating in the Prince William Sound. It is shipped cross-country to chill their Scotch with a bergy effervescence, releasing a sky that used to float above the dire wolf's brief dominion.

The True Dawn

Only a few times have I watched it rise out of the sea. Not the dawn of mountains or rolling plains — I mean the place where the light can start no lower. We've all seen sunsets above the water. They are not affected by the previous night's winc. They do not require us to be alarmed. We simply climb from the ocean and turn around, wiping our eyes and tasting the salt that has no hope of preserving us.

The Appendectomy Grin

There's a mark on my finger in the shape of Arkansas, but I can't recall when it first showed up. The blue dot in my forehead was a pencil point, and the appendectomy grin arrived in the usual manner. Some cultures encourage a decorative scarring; others value skin that has no wisdom. Regardless, your body is a story I cannot bear with so many buttons between us.

The 1970s

They began with the Beatles ending, and if you wanted to make a map, you needed two colors for Germany. It was a time of popsicles and flashlight tag, and while I was learning to multiply, the Japanese sea lion went extinct. I broke an arm. I started a coin collection. I noticed there were bats in the darkening air. Then, just as girls began to matter, they ended with a Soviet invasion.

History

It's funny how we pair up. Johannes Gutenberg will last as long as the Bible does, and Abraham Zapruder will ride into history with JFK. One thing is always attaching to the next, reminding me of tapeworms, of hermit crabs that curl into the dead and carry them. If we could reach far enough, we could figure out the sky. It is both easy and impossible. In the meantime, the lichens are gift-wrapping a boulder in our yard, waiting for the glacier to return for it.

I Used to Always Type Two Spaces After a Period

Now I hate those people — even though the impulse keeps returning, like the wish for a cigarette. The practice will eventually end. After all nobody says "thou" anymore, and the era of the stovepipe hat is never coming back. To have strong feelings about things that don't matter — it's an American luxury. The ice caps are converting into cities that will drown, but earlier today, I strained my back rearranging the room, to show off our new piano.

Pessimism

Fewer than fifty of Vermeer's paintings are cordoned by velvet ropes, and some of those are in dispute. The lilacs in our garden are pretty for just one week. You know what I'm saying. The moon is a coin above the reservoir, but you'll never get a chance to spend it.

The Problem With Calamities

Every day there is one less turkey in the field across our street. The calamities never stop happening and yet we are taken by surprise. The red salamanders, for instance, were plentiful as I headed down the trail. I couldn't stop finding them. But when I returned to the car I didn't see any, except for the ones I must have stepped on. The northern tooth fungus turns out to be photogenic, but that won't prevent it from killing your favorite tree. Be thankful for the breeze it cannot stop. Gather your shade while the maple still makes it.

Signature

Over the decades, it has grown less coherent, but everyone believes in this confusion of ink. Its unreadability proves that I am me.

A Practical Mortality

Anything can happen if I only hurry up. I pour a glass anyway. After all, the day I tried to tune the piano is the day I broke the piano, and it's been a while since anyone thought up a religion or a new sexual position. So many decisions and I am certain of nothing — except that I've abandoned *Infinite Jest* and I really don't feel bad.

The Smoke From California

You can only see the fog in somebody else's yard, and the horizon is most plentiful in the place it is farthest away. Wine gets better with age but only to a point, and a bottle is rarely opened at the moment of maximum pleasure. The smoke from California is improving my Connecticut sunset. From the back deck I can see my neighbor putting his yard to rights as the orange light keeps spreading in the oaks. I call inside for another glass of the cabernet. Meanwhile, the ivy on the side of our shed continues its ascent.

We Seldom Wish It

I was just outside enjoying the wind — the one that sent ships to Great Britain loaded with sugar and cotton. That's how long the pattern has persisted. Still, that doesn't stop the zebra mussels from clogging the intake pipe at the Stevenson Dam. The pattern can change, which is itself a pattern. One day a hawksbill turtle will show up at an island gone missing, and she will let loose her eggs in the open sea. What can be done? A new comet brightens in the sky above our house; a future tyrant is fussing in his crib. Something is always headed our way. We seldom wish it to hurry.

The Last Dinner

The stone I held was on the verge of being sand. The soul of a stone, really. That's what I'm interested in — the moment just before transubstantiation. A goose before it ripens into a North Face jacket. A balsam fir on the back of a truck on the way to becoming a Bible. I find a lot of broken dishes in the river that bisects our town. Nobody knows the last dinner that they held, and nobody really cares. But I wonder how much of this sandbar started out as tableware, how much of the air inside my house was once inside that cathedral.

The Problem With Conquistadors

I've seen them in paintings, trying not to fall into the Grand Canyon, and always they are wearing their armor, their metal helmets. It seems unlikely in that heat, and of course they had to turn back because, for days, they couldn't find a way to taste the water they'd been following. It wove through the rock without a sound — the channel getting deeper as, grain by grain, the desert set out for the sea.

I Like to Think of Myself as Having Goals

Someday, when I'm better, I'll dog paddle across the English Channel, I'll catalogue the spiders that have chosen to live inside with us. Until then, I'll keep stirring this broth counterclockwise, like the bats do the air above our yard where someone has all but drained the sky, as if its light were vodka.

Purses

Crocodile, ostrich, suckling calf — so many animals turn into purses. It is pointless to resist. After all the moon doesn't need a key to come inside, and I used to know a girl with bars across her windows. We have to make do. Some purses are built to fit a dictionary, while others can't accommodate Altoids. We carry the dead that carry what we need, and the snap that holds it all is golden.

From the Atheist's Handbook

1. As they are being burned, the saint and the atheist smell exactly the same.
2. Beware — any voice you hear coming across a great distance is likely your own echo.
3. The difference between religious and spiritual is the difference between airplane lights and stars.
4. A skeptic is someone whose wish to believe does not exceed his wish to be certain.
5. When the priest built the church, he made sure it had a door. How else to charge admission?

Each Morning the Piano Drifts Further Out of Tune

The shard of glass in the river today couldn't cut anything, and these wooden shelves don't remember the breeze of their last hillside. Our dog is on the mantel now. The urn is small — reminding me of when I first held a sequoia cone. Everything starts out this way — cancer, stamp collections. It's obvious now that barnacles attach to both container ship and whale. Look, a red-tailed hawk is passing over us, straddling the autumn we are standing in.

Optimism

After my appendectomy, there was one less way for me to die, and though the taffy pulled my filling out, I never stopped eating recklessly. I've heard that actors get better by playing the parts they didn't want, which explains the acceptance speech in my breast pocket. Nothing happens by chance. Even the executioner has a rationale for the order of our beheadings.

February

Every now and then I find a stinkbug inside the house. I can either flush it or throw it outside. I don't like my options, but I always take one. You can't open the windows in the Empire State Building, and yet there are spiders on the topmost floors. Some lice live only in the neck feathers of hummingbirds. We have to accept these miracles. Our garden is dead and the birds have abandoned us on a breeze of invisible wings.

Nothing Stays

The stars are never where you left them when you overstay the party. You know what I mean. We've all seen the famous migration of wildebeest, and, in theory at least, we understand the shiver of electrons inside a salad fork. Only the dam at Troy, New York, has kept the salt from rising northward. A pheasant is not open for inspection unless you've had it stuffed. Even then, it is not the same bird that surprised you in the corn. It is the warmth of a woman, left inside your bed, as she's picking up the things you had earlier removed.

Negative Capability

I don't actually want to figure out photons. We have named the thing that was confusing us, and that can be enough. Light is both particle and wave; love is both glory and pain. Keats could have been a physicist — he had the right temperament. He sang most clearly while coughing on his blood.

The Problem With Spring

First the trout lily, then the mint — and always in that order. Then suddenly the women in my office start showing up in short sleeves. I have to be careful while opening the porch umbrella. There's always a wasp inside, just getting started. Poison ivy, tax forms, April mud — the list gets longer and the sky contorts, making us believe this lazy creek might one day cause a canyon.

A Sweetness

The secret is to have no secrets. Be like the open bloom of anything — inspectable, without guile. The valley will let me look into it if I climb to the proper vantage. Nightly, the far-away sky discloses what I cannot comprehend. Still, confusion is a worthy goal if it conjures a sweetness that others can take away. Mothers and bees will understand me. I am one of those cups that cannot be carried without spilling a little wine.

This Is Your Only Warning

The peach is more forbidden. It can moisten your mouth just by thinking of it, and there is always a chance of flies. An apple, on the other hand, has never stained a cambric shirt. Even the core is edible, despite the small poisons hidden in the seeds. The peach has skin like ours, and can chip your teeth if you aren't careful. It has the heft of a planet pulled down from the sky, summoning the kiss you cannot refuse.

Coreopsis

It’s a perennial so it keeps coming back like nervous breakdowns and Presidents’ Day sales. Its seeds are the color of dirt, and I’d never have guessed they’d keep the side of our house so yellow, even when the weather is dry. It has not been dry. For weeks, we’ve alternated between downpour and drizzly overcast. I’ve been staying on the couch, watching the news and failing to finish every novel that I start — confident of nothing but these little flames the rains seem only to fan.

Selling Points

I'm sure the neighbors want this corner cleared away, but the goldenrod is full of bees and the wind is plucking at a crown of thistle. It should come as no surprise that I'm rooting for mayhem, the ability of things that live here, to live here. On the edge of our lawn, at least, it doesn't take long for the cardinals to disappear. True, with all these trees, the gutters clog twice a year. But inside the garage I've left you a ladder to keep the cool rain moving.

The Problem With Not Owning a Ladder

People head home under all sorts of circumstances — the road made blurry by a third glass of wine or dirty wipers, a child who won't stop kicking. Earlier today I saw a man with so many balloons inside his car I was afraid he'd cause an accident. Now I can't stop thinking about the jaws of life, how if they pried apart his car, the balloons would hurry skyward. Some people prefer that kind of showmanship. They like the idea of their birthday wish snagged on this high, unreachable branch.

Seahorse

This oak leaf has a hole in the shape of a seahorse. There is no explanation you can give me that will make it seem less terrible. That's the kind of mood I'm in. It's the male seahorse that gives birth. The proud fathers latch onto the grasses as their children drift away. As you might have guessed, the world eats most of them, and at this time of year, there's some kind of hole in almost every leaf.

The Problem With Glaciers

Sometimes the big things are missing. I'm thinking of runaway fathers and DDT. Just yesterday I saw a dozen eagles, and the ice here was once a mile thick. There's a reason the landscape dips and crumbles and fills to the ankle with swamp. We've learned to walk slowly through it, to use a staff when crossing the river — each of us believing that his daughter will forgive him, that he'll somehow keep his footing as the Earth rolls out and away.

On the Back Patio With Bach and Whiskey While Waiting for the Perseids

I used to look up into the night sky and wish for more stars. Such audacity — the dissatisfaction with infinity, the certainty I could have done better.

A Song on the Radio

When you think of her now, she's like a song on the radio you've heard too often. Time and again you keep on listening, believing you're near the end.

The Terrible Part

The bittersweet doesn't need my permission to strangle the cherry tree beside the shed. The clearness of a creek will last as long as I stay out of it. The world gets on without me — that's the terrible part. One day the cicada grows tired of living on underground sap. Then suddenly it is breaking out of its own back, amazed at the air, shouting into the summer heat like it's almost out of time.

Now We Are Planning a Party

Every 17 years the cicadas rise up and make it hard to hear the radio. Nothing wants to stay hidden. The booby trap, the tumor — they all have a way of announcing themselves. I still remember the phone number of the house where I first ate Salisbury steak, and later, when we came to this one, how the basement filled with all that we thought we'd never need. In one of these boxes — the rumor of your mother's china.

Cougar

The cougar had traveled all the way from South Dakota before it died in Connecticut on the Wilbur Cross Parkway. Having come so far to be destroyed, it reminds me of American soldiers marching across the countries of Asia, or the dust of comets igniting in the air above my patio. Somewhere, another cougar is picking up the scent and making the trek, ending in ink that has somehow dried in the shape of the poem before you.

A Life of Proportionate Water

This flood, from any distance, looks like every other — the same mud in the living room, the same canoes rescuing the elderly. A happy life is a life of proportionate water. The same could be said of money and cold sores. In South Jersey, the pines give way to oaks if someone keeps putting the fires out. Thus I've driven down many roads with a different forest on either side, making me feel like a fulcrum. I'm here to say that feeling doesn't last. You can't read a book that's been underwater, and the corn, once withered, has never once come back.

The Silence of the Marriage

The silence of the marriage continued to solidify, and no one mentioned it. In the same way, we fail to notice the growth of trees, though it is happening even as we look at them — or the way that paint hardens in a can imperfectly sealed against the air we are always breathing. On a day like this, the cherries float over us like dark stars, and the breeze smells of foxes. It's then that I notice how the cabinets need retouching, how the separate notes inside of us have gathered to a chord.

The Problem With Loosestrife

I can't get over to that purple flower without trampling all this goldenrod — to say nothing of the damaged ants, the flushed tanagers. This is the way it's always been. I see what I want and the world allows me to harm it in pursuit. Look, there's the raccoon I ran over on the way to your house last weekend. And over here, hanging on a hook, the leather jacket that defines my middle age. Desire is a coin I've always spent. The moon floats over in a rage of brightness as if that could keep it safe.

Manifesto

I want the world to change and to stay exactly as it is. Anyone who disagrees must never have held one woman while thinking of another. There's talk of cloning the mammoth, and the seed vaults of Norway continue to fill with the hardiest strains of lemongrass. I still remember the day my daughter came home to say that she'd never learn cursive. It was one of many moments. Outside, the forsythia has defined the borders of our yard. Look hard. Even as I wait for the coffee to drip, those bushes are blurring with the grass I'll soon be cutting.

Separation

Part of Connecticut used to touch Africa, and when I push through the bushes on the edge of our pond, the turtles click like poker chips off of their muddy logs. Wherever I am, the world makes room, despite the roots and boulders. Every year, the moon floats 1.5 inches farther away from us, and on the other side of the planet, the wildebeest approach a river full of crocodiles. Fear or desire — it doesn't matter which. The cameraman presses record.

The Problem With the Washington Monument

It was the tallest structure in the world for only five years. The Great Pyramid of Giza held that title for thousands. The records keep getting broken of course, only faster. When I was a boy, I played baseball with someone whose father got a medal for being quick. He was fat when I met him; he had a limp. The history books once lamented the burning of a single library. The idea of Dresden had yet to occur.

There Was a Time When I Might Have Thrown Away This Sheet Music

I never learned to play but now it's vintage, so we continue to let it yellow inside the piano bench, doubling as a stand for our spider plants, a store-bought conch. Neckties are another matter. Even funerals don't insist. They are going the way of the bowler hat and the monocle. Some things you let go of, thinking they're gone for good, but when I'm in the woods of my town, in the farthest reaches of it, the trash I'm most likely to come across is a Mylar balloon that a child set forth, believing it might visit the chalk mark of the moon.

Oxbows

Curves in the river keep breaking off as it heads to the sea's address. They do their best to be what they've become, and we admire them for it, if only because of the mallard eggs, which their banks can hold without breaking. These lakes fill in with silt and cattails, transitioning over the decades to bog and pasture. Listen — the bell of some future dairy cow is clanking on the wind as it returns to a barn that is still a bunch of trees, their branches full of finches on the way to someplace warm.

Underneath I-84

The cicadas are coming soon, arriving like the need to replace a hot water tank. Growing up, we had a cuckoo clock that ran a little slow, and the church bells made us think about damnation. Starlight is the best measure — I've always felt a chill as Orion rose out of the trees. The rivers continue to freeze and thaw, and the swallows return to my personal Capistrano, after the mint has risen.

On Being Told I Write Too Much About the Moon

The sun shatters on the windy lake and everyone agrees it's lovely. I can't help it. The scene would be more moving if the moon hung there instead. I could spend all night watching those fragments fail to reassemble. O bright blister, O cigarette hole in negative, O ghostly dime, O albino quesadilla — we have never known exactly what you mean, but even the worst of us look up at you and pause.

The Case Against the Semicolon

1. It is one foot on the platform and the other foot on the train.
2. It is part of the wink emoji.
3. It is twilight.
4. It is the length of time between when you stopped kissing me and when you felt relief.
5. It is Wednesday.
6. It is shale when the world wanted mud or slate.
7. It is the pause between Netflix episodes.
8. It is too much and too little at once.
9. It has never been used in a love letter.

In Praise of the Invisible

Every marble statue started out as seashells. I don't care if you can't see them. Likewise, this cherry pie began as bees forcing their faces in for the droplet of nectar. You'd be surprised how little the world is willing to surrender. I just saw a hummingbird singing for the first time and I'm 54. I still haven't read Proust, and it occurs to me that I've opened the glove compartments of only a dozen cars. Imagine the pistols and outdated maps, the bottles of something saved for later. All the while, the mine fire of your kiss continues beneath this landscape of suburbs and rolling hills.

When I Was Twenty

The problems I had have all been solved or turned out not to be problems. We're all takers is what I'm saying — even the flowers. Some of them won't open till late afternoon, hoarding a nectar they can only give away. Back then, there was no such thing as a mortgage. We fought about the record player, and everyone smoked. The idea of our dying was a distant storm, turning atop an ocean on somebody else's map.

The Problem With Philosophers

I spend a lot of time on distinctions — whether I prefer compulsions or obsessions, whether *outer space* or *firmament* is better for what's above. *Meadowlarks* and *dungeons* are another matter. Now that I've written them into a sentence, I'll think of them both whenever just one is mentioned. At a dinner party, no one is eager to sit beside a philosopher. They are always into their third glass of wine, and everyone is hoping the baked Alaska might settle the conversation.

I No Longer Worry About Drowning in Misnamed Water

Some days I can't tell the difference between a treble clef and an ampersand. I confuse the silhouettes of raven and crow. I say phooey to distinctions. Planet or star, it is just a light that will disappear — snuffed by a blueness of the blazing day. If the lake is big enough, it looks like an ocean, but the taste of it won't matter. Whatever boat you cross it in will kill you when it sinks.

Appendix

This is where the tangents live on — all those things the author couldn't bear to do without. They smell unnecessary — like cologne dabbed onto the neck of a man fighting brush fires. Cologne is also the birthplace of men's perfume. The shop that formulated Eau de Cologne in 1709 is still open, after surviving 262 bombing raids during World War II. The scent is also referenced in the lyrics of *Quadrophenia*, a double album by the Who released in 1973, not long after my first encounter with pornography.

The Family's Button Supply

This weather used to be in Asia, and in the olden days, I would have gotten a scapula from the butcher and left it in the sun — that was the family's button supply. As with lice and measles, everything comes from someplace else. Take these birds dotting the branches of this otherwise empty tree. They look like inverted pears. But they all started out as eggs, and no one can find their unraveling nests in the bushes that divide our yards. Now that cloud, in the shape of a dead peasant, is on its way to Europe.

Babel

God tore down the Tower of Babel because he didn't like the work. Now the Frenchman and the Mongolian have everything in common, except for the way they shape their mouths to describe the world before them. Despite the difficulties, the towers have kept on rising — in Shanghai, New York, Mecca. They are so high that, if you fell off of one, you could say a whole prayer before hitting the street. Think about it. We are heading back to the moon, and our telescopes can almost see the beginning now. In the paper today, someone has brought a toddler to the lobby of Mount Everest.

Nitrogen

The gas makes up most of what we breathe. Apparently, it's here to keep the world from exploding when I light a cigarette. How else to understand the Apollo disaster? Likewise, I try to make sense of the ball of molten metal at the center of our planet. Both everything and nothing seem fine on this side of the eggshell. Despite the asteroids and tsunamis, we carry on. Look, we are saving the tiger by giving it a cage.

Newtown

We brag about our corn maze, the fact our fields still accommodate some cows. It's hard to believe we're known mostly for mass murder. It's even harder to believe the shooting will one day fail to define us. On holiday weekends, the Boy Scouts set out coffee for the drunks and tired drivers. We have a dog park, occasional bears, a giant flag in the middle of the highway. The cell service is always good and the goose shit deepens in the Ram Pasture pond. As you might have guessed, the water is both pretty and undrinkable.

Heaven

Such an extravagance — to believe we're owed an eternity, even as we squander the gift of the present. When our children were young, I made a point of not mentioning heaven. I wanted their goodness to be its own reward. I wanted them to understand the limits of ripeness. Then their grandmother died, and the old lie came naturally to my lips, the way a bird will copy the song of its parents — even though the nest has unraveled, even though the tree that held it lies stacked in a corner of a chilly room.

Salamanders

Someday I'll learn to pay attention to salamanders. Until then they must continue beneath their logs, like a sport that no one follows. I have to believe there's time. After all, the colonists eventually stopped sounding like the British. For my own part, I've begun writing "possum" instead of "opossum," and just last week, I was able to remove an orange peel as a single fragrant husk.

An Omelet for the Sedges

Let's say you were a wild egg, that she lifted you out of the prairie grass before a wall of advancing flame. She prevented the premature hatching; she saved you from becoming an omelet for the sedges. Of course you missed the sense of rustling carried past you on the wind, but you learned to love the old sweater inside the Amazon box, the reading lamp she bent above you and never switched off. It burned her once when she leaned in close to check on you — waiting for the yolk to coalesce, for the hook of your beak to enter her side, the place you have come to call everything.

Disappointments

The lovemaking reminded her of a bad piano lesson, and the quality of sunshine filling the trees didn't go well with her outfit. There was always something to be improved — that was the real problem. When she finally made it to the front of the crowd, the Mona Lisa was smaller than she had hoped. Conversely, the Grand Canyon was too grand. She couldn't fit it all inside of her, and she was left with the blandness of ordinary stars burning in a sky she could not revise.

Cold Vodka

It was April and I drove over a frog on the way home from work. Later, on the back deck, I wanted to listen to the silence of the dripping woods, but all I could hear was my own tinnitus. Once again, the auroras failed to reach down to Connecticut. Once again, I was left with cold vodka and the brightness of named stars. That's when I remembered a piece of advice I had meant to give my daughter, but she was abroad in a city with different traffic patterns. If you've ever dropped something off the side of a boat by accident, you know exactly how I felt.

Persistence

For example, a redwood became my late neighbor's picnic table, which his daughter set out on the lawn to display his fedoras. He had worn them as a young man, she said. Each hat had a bright feather stuck in the band. They didn't look like they came from the birds around here, and nobody wanted the hats. Even so, the picnic table got loaded into a truck before the dew burned off, and the hats are now part of a poem.

Amazon Bonsai

The juniper has a hunkered look, as if it were withstanding a storm we could not hear. In the olden days, bonsai were passed down from one generation to the next, like a propensity for mental illness. Now we have free shipping; now we have citalopram. Even so, our bookshelf has always been windless, and the wild profusion of the spider plants feels like mockery, as I lift the tree from its tiny tray and clip away its roots. Outside, the willows play havoc with our septic system, and the maples unbuckle the sidewalk squares of the oldest street in town.

The Smoke Rose Out of Manhattan

While Connecticut sent its fire engines south, the sky remained blue and full of birdsong. That's why I don't trust pictures of people in hammocks beside clear water. In the hospital, we did our best to keep the TV off. We focused on milk and diapers, and why our baby was yellow. By the time our daughter made it home, they still hadn't put the fire out. She recently stopped asking for gas money, and she is headed to college now. On the other side of the world, above the liberated lands, the presidents must fly by night and unannounced.

The Last American Slave Died in 1972

I could have passed Peter Mills in my baby carriage if my parents ever took me to Pittsburgh. It's something to think about — that the Beatles broke up before the last slave had died. Race suffuses everything, though my whiteness can make it hard to see, as I stand outside my home without anyone asking if it's mine. True, my lack of melanin leaves me prone to skin cancer but also to better paychecks. And when the police arrive, I am confident the phone I called them on won't come to resemble a pistol. I understand my privilege. I'm so white that if I were black I'd expect a different world.

The Problem With Latin

The Romans were great once too. Now the empire endures as a collection of tourist traps, a subject taught at prep schools. Even after the sacking of Rome, the language kept spreading like wine across a tablecloth. People still use it for mottos. We have a scrap of it on our money. The rest of it has disappeared or hidden itself inside the words we call our own. At this late stage, I'm more likely to learn the harpsichord. If I need to know what Catullus thought of Flavius, I'll read it in translation.

Poetry

1. Trusting a poem is our first mistake. Living as if we had not heard it is the second.
2. In a forest, the best poets think of axe handles and violins.
3. Poetry is like the moon. It can only help you see if you're in the dark already.
4. A good poet is like a vulture. He relies on the tongue to tell him what has value. He takes the roadkill of August and transforms it into flight.
5. A poem should have meaning the way the stars have meaning — not as something explainable, but as something irrefutable.

The Land of Steady Decline

I can't do a cartwheel anymore, and like everyone else, I waste a lot of time on Facebook. The only thing I've learned there is that the beauties of high school have all turned into Republicans. It's a shame. I doubt that anyone will tune this piano. Like the dog, it has been in steady decline. I'm no arborist so I didn't know how to trim this tree without killing it. Now its branches are in the power lines, and no one will hold the ladder.

The Strength of American Wishes

To make a better postcard, someone dug a tunnel into the redwood and let a car pass through. We can't do that anymore — just like we can't find a passenger pigeon. They died out because of our wish to always hit something when firing a gun. Comebacks can happen though. Think of that photograph of bison skulls piled higher than a house. We went from 60 million animals in 1800 to 541 in 1889. Now we are raising them for steak and dogfood. Now we are making our money.

Acknowledgments

Thank you to the following publications in which some of these poems first appeared:

Alaska Quarterly Review: "The Problem With Glaciers";
The Banyan Review: "A Song on the Radio," "There Was a Time When I Might Have Thrown Away This Sheet Music";
Bennington Review: "Salamanders," "Disappointments," "Poetry";
Best Small Fictions, 2023: "The Problem With Mutability";
Bracken: "Newtown";
California Quarterly: "Purses," "The 1970s," "I Like to Think of Myself as Having Goals";
Citron Review: "The Problem With Not Owning a Ladder";
Cola Literary Review: "I Am Not Without Hope";
Comstock Review: "The 1970s," "American Bonsai";
Connecticut River Review: "A Love Poem of Sorts," "The Problem With Latin";
Copper Nickel: "The Silence of the Marriage";

Diaphanous Micro: "Nitrogen," "The Case Against the Semicolon," "Cold Vodka," "The Last American Slave Died in 1972," "Signature," "The Problem With Philosophers";

Eastern Iowa Review: "I No Longer Worry About Drowning in Misnamed Water," "An Omelet for the Sedges";

8 Poems: "The Problem With Loosestrife";

Gargoyle: "The Land of Steady Decline";

Harpur Palate: "The Smoke Rose Out of Manhattan";

Inkwell Journal: "When I Was Twenty";

L=Y=R=A: "The Problem With Conquistadors," "The Problem With Luxury," "From the Atheist's Handbook";

Mason Street: "The Family's Button Supply";

Neologism Poetry Journal: "In Praise of the Invisible";

New World Writing: "Negative Capability," "On the Back Patio With Bach and Whiskey While Waiting for the Perseids";

The Night Heron Barks: "On Being Told I Write Too Much About the Moon," "Separation," "Pessimism," "Now We Are Planning a Party";

Paperbark: "A Life of Proportionate Water";

Pithead Chapel: "Coreopsis," "This Is Your Only Warning," "Selling Points";
Ploughshares: "Manifesto";
Poetry Is Currency: "The Problem With the Washington Monument," "A Sweetness";
Ran Off With the Star Bassoon: "Nothing Stays";
Red Noise Collective: "The True Dawn";
South Florida Poetry Journal: "A Practical Mortality";
The Southern Review: "The Problem With Spring," "Each Morning the Piano Drifts Further Out of Tune," "February," "Optimism," "Conversation Piece," "The Strength of American Wishes," "The Problem With Maps," "The Problem With Mutability," "Seahorse," "I Used to Always Type Two Spaces After a Period," "The Last Dinner," "We Seldom Wish It," "The Problem With Calamities," "The Smoke From California";
2River: "Persistence," "Oxbows";
Untenured: "Cougar";
Verse Daily: "The Silence of the Marriage," "The Problem With Maps";
The Westchester Review: "The Terrible Part."

About the Author

Charles Rafferty is the author of 15 poetry books and chapbooks, most recently *A Cluster of Noisy Planets* (BOA Editions, 2021). His poems have appeared in *The New Yorker*, *O, Oprah Magazine*, *The Southern Review*, *Gettysburg Review*, *Poetry Daily*, *Verse Daily*, *Rhino*, *Prairie Schooner*, and *Ploughshares*. His stories have been collected in *Saturday Night at Magellan's* (Fomite Press, 2013) and *Somebody Who Knows Somebody* (Gold Wake Press, 2021). He has also published a novel, *Moscodelphia* (Woodhall Press, 2021). Rafferty has received grants from the National Endowment for the Arts and the Connecticut Commission on the Arts. Currently, he is a director at a research and advisory firm. Rafferty is also a songwriter and a naturalist. He prefers the river to the sea.

BOA Editions, Ltd. American Poets Continuum Series

No. 1 *The Fuhrer Bunker: A Cycle of Poems in Progress*
W. D. Snodgrass

No. 2 *She*
M. L. Rosenthal

No. 3 *Living With Distance*
Ralph J. Mills, Jr.

No. 4 *Not Just Any Death*
Michael Waters

No. 5 *That Was Then: New and Selected Poems*
Isabella Gardner

No. 6 *Things That Happen Where There Aren't Any People*
William Stafford

No. 7 *The Bridge of Change: Poems 1974–1980*
John Logan

No. 8 *Signatures*
Joseph Stroud

No. 9 *People Live Here: Selected Poems 1949–1983*
Louis Simpson

No. 10 *Yin*
Carolyn Kizer

No. 11 *Duhamel: Ideas of Order in Little Canada*
Bill Tremblay

No. 12 *Seeing It Was So*
Anthony Piccione

No. 13 *Hyam Plutzik: The Collected Poems*

No. 14 *Good Woman: Poems and a Memoir 1969–1980*
Lucille Clifton

No. 15 *Next: New Poems*
Lucille Clifton

No. 16 *Roxa: Voices of the Culver Family*
William B. Patrick

No. 17 *John Logan: The Collected Poems*

No. 18 *Isabella Gardner: The Collected Poems*

No. 19 *The Sunken Lightship*
Peter Makuck

No. 20 *The City in Which I Love You*
Li-Young Lee

No. 21 *Quilting: Poems 1987–1990*
Lucille Clifton

No. 22 *John Logan: The Collected Fiction*

No. 23 *Shenandoah and Other Verse Plays*
Delmore Schwartz

No. 24 *Nobody Lives on Arthur Godfrey Boulevard*
Gerald Costanzo

No. 25 *The Book of Names: New and Selected Poems*
Barton Sutter

No. 26 *Each in His Season*
W. D. Snodgrass

No. 27 *Wordworks: Poems Selected and New*
Richard Kostelanetz

No. 28 *What We Carry*
Dorianne Laux

No. 29 *Red Suitcase*
Naomi Shihab Nye

No. 30 *Song*
Brigit Pegeen Kelly

No. 31 *The Fuehrer Bunker: The Complete Cycle*
W. D. Snodgrass

No. 32 *For the Kingdom*
Anthony Piccione

No. 33 *The Quicken Tree*
Bill Knott

No. 34 *These Upraised Hands*
William B. Patrick

No. 35 *Crazy Horse in Stillness*
William Heyen

No. 36 *Quick, Now, Always*
Mark Irwin

No. 37 *I Have Tasted the Apple*
Mary Crow

No. 38 *The Terrible Stories*
Lucille Clifton

No. 39 *The Heat of Arrivals*
Ray Gonzalez

No. 40 *Jimmy & Rita*
Kim Addonizio

No. 41 *Green Ash, Red Maple, Black Gum*
Michael Waters

No. 42 *Against Distance*
Peter Makuck

No. 43 *The Night Path*
Laurie Kutchins

No. 44 *Radiography*
Bruce Bond

No. 45 *At My Ease: Uncollected Poems of the Fifties and Sixties*
David Ignatow

No. 46 *Trillium*
Richard Foerster

No. 47 *Fuel*
Naomi Shihab Nye

No. 48 *Gratitude*
Sam Hamill

No. 49 *Diana, Charles, & the Queen*
William Heyen

No. 50 *Plus Shipping*
Bob Hicok

No. 51 *Cabato Sentora*
Ray Gonzalez

No. 52 *We Didn't Come Here for This*
William B. Patrick

No. 53 *The Vandals*
Alan Michael Parker

No. 54 *To Get Here*
Wendy Mnookin

No. 55 *Living Is What I Wanted: Last Poems*
David Ignatow

No. 56 *Dusty Angel*
Michael Blumenthal

No. 57 *The Tiger Iris*
Joan Swift

No. 58 *White City*
Mark Irwin

No. 59 *Laugh at the End of the World: Collected Comic Poems 1969–1999*
Bill Knott

No. 60 *Blessing the Boats: New and Selected Poems: 1988–2000*
Lucille Clifton

No. 61 *Tell Me*
Kim Addonizio

No. 62 *Smoke*
Dorianne Laux

No. 63 *Parthenopi: New and Selected Poems*
Michael Waters

No. 64 *Rancho Notorious*
Richard Garcia

No. 65 *Jam*
Joe-Anne McLaughlin

No. 66 *A. Poulin, Jr. Selected Poems*
Edited, with an Introduction by Michael Waters

No. 67 *Small Gods of Grief*
Laure-Anne Bosselaar

No. 68 *Book of My Nights*
Li-Young Lee

No. 69 *Tulip Farms and Leper Colonies*
Charles Harper Webb

No. 70 *Double Going*
Richard Foerster

No. 71 *What He Took*
Wendy Mnookin

No. 72 *The Hawk Temple at Tierra Grande*
Ray Gonzalez

No. 73 *Mules of Love*
Ellen Bass

No. 74 *The Guests at the Gate*
Anthony Piccione

No. 75 *Dumb Luck*
Sam Hamill

No. 76 *Love Song with Motor Vehicles*
Alan Michael Parker

No. 77 *Life Watch*
Willis Barnstone

No. 78 *The Owner of the House: New Collected Poems 1940–2001*
Louis Simpson

No. 79 *Is*
Wayne Dodd

No. 80 *Late*
Cecilia Woloch

No. 81 *Precipitates*
Debra Kang Dean

No. 82 *The Orchard*
Brigit Pegeen Kelly

No. 83 *Bright Hunger*
Mark Irwin

No. 84 *Desire Lines: New and Selected Poems*
Lola Haskins

No. 85 *Curious Conduct*
Jeanne Marie Beaumont

No. 86 *Mercy*
Lucille Clifton

No. 87 *Model Homes*
Wayne Koestenbaum

No. 88 *Farewell to the Starlight in Whiskey*
Barton Sutter

No. 89 *Angels for the Burning*
David Mura

No. 90 *The Rooster's Wife*
Russell Edson

No. 91 *American Children*
Jim Simmerman

No. 92 *Postcards from the Interior*
Wyn Cooper

No. 93 *You & Yours*
Naomi Shihab Nye

No. 94 *Consideration of the Guitar: New and Selected Poems 1986–2005*
Ray Gonzalez

No. 95 *Off-Season in the Promised Land*
Peter Makuck

No. 96 *The Hoopoe's Crown*
Jacqueline Osherow

No. 97 *Not for Specialists: New and Selected Poems*
W. D. Snodgrass

No. 98 *Splendor*
Steve Kronen

No. 99 *Woman Crossing a Field*
Deena Linett

No. 100 *The Burning of Troy*
Richard Foerster

No. 101 *Darling Vulgarity*
Michael Waters

No. 102 *The Persistence of Objects*
Richard Garcia

No. 103 *Slope of the Child Everlasting*
Laurie Kutchins

No. 104 *Broken Hallelujahs*
Sean Thomas Dougherty

No. 105 *Peeping Tom's Cabin: Comic Verse 1928–2008*
X. J. Kennedy

No. 106 *Disclamor*
G.C. Waldrep

No. 107 *Encouragement for a Man Falling to His Death*
Christopher Kennedy

No. 108 *Sleeping with Houdini*
Nin Andrews

No. 109 *Nomina*
Karen Volkman

No. 110 *The Fortieth Day*
Kazim Ali

No. 111 *Elephants & Butterflies*
Alan Michael Parker

No. 112 *Voices*
Lucille Clifton

No. 113 *The Moon Makes Its Own Plea*
Wendy Mnookin

No. 114 *The Heaven-Sent Leaf*
Katy Lederer

No. 115 *Struggling Times*
Louis Simpson

No. 116 *And*
Michael Blumenthal

No. 117 *Carpathia*
Cecilia Woloch

No. 118 *Seasons of Lotus, Seasons of Bone*
Matthew Shenoda

No. 119 *Sharp Stars*
Sharon Bryan

No. 120 *Cool Auditor*
Ray Gonzalez

No. 121 *Long Lens: New and Selected Poems*
Peter Makuck

No. 122 *Chaos Is the New Calm*
Wyn Cooper

No. 123 *Diwata*
Barbara Jane Reyes

No. 124 *Burning of the Three Fires*
Jeanne Marie Beaumont

No. 125 *Sasha Sings the Laundry on the Line*
Sean Thomas Dougherty

No. 126 *Your Father on the Train of Ghosts*
G.C. Waldrep and John Gallaher

No. 127 *Ennui Prophet*
Christopher Kennedy

No. 128 *Transfer*
Naomi Shihab Nye

No. 129 *Gospel Night*
Michael Waters

No. 130 *The Hands of Strangers: Poems from the Nursing Home*
Janice N. Harrington

No. 131 *Kingdom Animalia*
Aracelis Girmay

No. 132 *True Faith*
Ira Sadoff

No. 133 *The Reindeer Camps and Other Poems*
Barton Sutter

No. 134 *The Collected Poems of Lucille Clifton: 1965–2010*

No. 135 *To Keep Love Blurry*
Craig Morgan Teicher

No. 136 *Theophobia*
Bruce Beasley

No. 137 *Refuge*
Adrie Kusserow

No. 138 *The Book of Goodbyes*
Jillian Weise

No. 139 *Birth Marks*
Jim Daniels

No. 140 *No Need of Sympathy*
Fleda Brown

No. 141 *There's a Box in the Garage You Can Beat with a Stick*
Michael Teig

No. 142 *The Keys to the Jail*
Keetje Kuipers

No. 143 *All You Ask for Is Longing: New and Selected Poems 1994–2014*
Sean Thomas Dougherty

No. 144 *Copia*
Erika Meitner

No. 145 *The Chair: Prose Poems*
Richard Garcia

No. 146 *In a Landscape*
John Gallaher

No. 147 *Fanny Says*
Nickole Brown

No. 148 *Why God Is a Woman*
Nin Andrews

No. 149 *Testament*
G.C. Waldrep

No. 150 *I'm No Longer Troubled by the Extravagance*
Rick Bursky

No. 151 *Antidote for Night*
Marsha de la O

No. 152 *Beautiful Wall*
Ray Gonzalez

No. 153 *the black maria*
Aracelis Girmay

No. 154 *Celestial Joyride*
Michael Waters

No. 155 *Whereso*
Karen Volkman

No. 156 *The Day's Last Light Reddens the Leaves of the Copper Beech*
Stephen Dobyns

No. 157 *The End of Pink*
Kathryn Nuernberger

No. 158 *Mandatory Evacuation*
Peter Makuck

No. 159 *Primitive: The Art and Life of Horace H. Pippin*
Janice N. Harrington

No. 160 *The Trembling Answers*
Craig Morgan Teicher

No. 161 *Bye-Bye Land*
Christian Barter

No. 162 *Sky Country*
Christine Kitano

No. 163 *All Soul Parts Returned*
Bruce Beasley

No. 164 *The Smoke of Horses*
Charles Rafferty

No. 165 *The Second O of Sorrow*
Sean Thomas Dougherty

No. 166 *Holy Moly Carry Me*
Erika Meitner

No. 167 *Clues from the Animal Kingdom*
Christopher Kennedy

No. 168 *Dresses from the Old Country*
Laura Read

No. 169 *In Country*
Hugh Martin

No. 170 *The Tiny Journalist*
Naomi Shihab Nye

No. 171 *All Its Charms*
Keetje Kuipers

No. 172 *Night Angler*
Geffrey Davis

No. 173 *The Human Half*
Deborah Brown

No. 174 *Cyborg Detective*
Jillian Weise

No. 175 *On the Shores of Welcome Home*
Bruce Weigl

No. 176 *Rue*
Kathryn Nuernberger

No. 177 *Let's Become a Ghost Story*
Rick Bursky

No. 178 *Year of the Dog*
Deborah Paredez

No. 179 *Brand New Spacesuit*
John Gallaher

No. 180 *How to Carry Water: Selected Poems of Lucille Clifton*
Edited, with an Introduction by Aracelis Girmay

No. 181 *Caw*
Michael Waters

No. 182 *Letters to a Young Brown Girl*
Barbara Jane Reyes

No. 183 *Mother Country*
Elana Bell

No. 184 *Welcome to Sonnetville, New Jersey*
Craig Morgan Teicher

No. 185 *I Am Not Trying to Hide My Hungers from the World*
Kendra DeColo

No. 186 *The Naomi Letters*
Rachel Mennies

No. 187 *Tenderness*
Derrick Austin

No. 188 *Ceive*
B.K. Fischer

No. 189 *Diamonds*
Camille Guthrie

No. 190 *A Cluster of Noisy Planets*
Charles Rafferty

No. 191 *Useful Junk*
Erika Meitner

No. 192 *Field Notes from the Flood Zone*
Heather Sellers

No. 193 *A Season in Hell with Rimbaud*
Dustin Pearson

No. 194 *Your Emergency Contact Has Experienced an Emergency*
Chen Chen

No. 195 *A Tinderbox in Three Acts*
Cynthia Dewi Oka

No. 196 *Little Mr. Prose Poem: Selected Poems of Russell Edson*
Edited by Craig Morgan Teicher

No. 197 *The Dug-Up Gun Museum*
Matt Donovan

No. 198 *Four in Hand*
Alicia Mountain

No. 199 *Buffalo Girl*
Jessica Q. Stark

No. 200 *Nomenclatures of Invisibility*
Mahtem Shiferraw

No. 201 *Flare, Corona*
Jeannine Hall Gailey

No. 202 *Death Prefers the Minor Keys*
Sean Thomas Dougherty

No. 203 *Desire Museum*
Danielle Deulen

No. 204 *Transitory*
Subhaga Crystal Bacon

No. 205 *Every Hard Sweetness*
Sheila Carter-Jones

No. 206 *Blue on a Blue Palette*
Lynne Thompson

No. 207 *One Wild Word Away*
Geffrey Davis

No. 208 *The Strange God Who Makes Us*
Christopher Kennedy

No. 209 *Our Splendid Failure to Do the Impossible*
Rebecca Lindenberg

No. 210 *Yard Show*
Janice N. Harrington

No. 211 *The Last Song of the World*
Joseph Fasano

No. 212 *Lonely Women Make Good Lovers*
Keetje Kuipers

No. 213 *jump the gun*
Jennie Malboeuf

No. 214 *Apostle of Desire*
Bruce Weigl

No. 215 *GREEN OF ALL HEADS*
Aracelis Girmay

No. 216 *Pluck*
Adam Hughes

No. 217 *Disaster Tourism*
Rena J. Mosteirin

No. 218 *The Appendectomy Grin*
Charles Rafferty

Colophon

BOA Editions, Ltd., a nonprofit publisher of poetry and other literary works, fosters readership and appreciation of contemporary literature. By identifying, cultivating, and publishing both new and established poets and selecting authors of unique literary talent, BOA brings high-quality literature to the public.

Support for this effort comes from the sale of its publications, grant funding, and private donations.

❋

The publication of this book is made possible, in part, by the special support of the following individuals:

Anonymous (x2)
Ralph Black & Susan Murphy
Angela Bonazinga & Catherine Lewis
Gwen Conners, *in memory of June Baker*
Chris Dahl, *in honor of Chuck Hertrick*
David Fraher, *in memory of A. Poulin Jr.*
Bonnie Garner
Carol Godsave
James Hale

Nora A. Jones
Christopher Kennedy
Joe & Dale Klein
Jack & Gail Langerak
Barbara Lovenheim, *in memory of John Lovenheim*
Joe McElveney
John & Judy Messenger
Dorrie Parini
Boo Poulin, *in memory of A. Poulin Jr.*
Michael Quattrone
Deborah Ronnen
John H. Schultz
William Waddell & Linda Rubel